YOU CHOOSE™
BOOKS

The Race to the MOON

An Interactive History Adventure

by Allison Lassieur

Consultant:
Suezette Rene Bieri
Education Program Coordinator, Retired
Department of Space Studies and School of Aerospace Sciences
University of North Dakota

CAPSTONE PRESS
a capstone imprint

You Choose Books are published by Capstone Press,
1710 Roe Crest Drive, North Mankato, Minnesota 56003
www.capstonepub.com

Library of Congress Cataloging-in-Publication Data
Lassieur, Allison.
The race to the moon: an interactive history adventure / by Allison Lassieur.
 pages cm – (You choose. History.)
Audience: Ages 8-12.
Audience: Grade 4 to 6.
Summary: "Describes the space race and the moon landing. Readers' choices reveal
various historical details"— Provided by publisher.
Includes bibliographical references and index.
ISBN 978-1-4765-4185-3 (library binding)
ISBN 978-1-4765-5216-3 (paperback)
ISBN 978-1-4765-6062-5 (eBook PDF)
1. Space race—History—Juvenile literature. 2. Astronautics—United States—
History—Juvenile literature. 3. Astronautics—Soviet Union—History—Juvenile
literature. 4. Project Apollo (U.S.)—Juvenile literature. 5. Space flight to the
moon—History—Juvenile literature. I. Title.
TL793.L294 2014
629.45,4—dc23   2013035318

Editorial Credits
Brenda Haugen, editor; Bobbie Nuytten, designer; Wanda Winch, media researcher;
Danielle Ceminsky, production specialist

Photo Credits
AP Images, 49, NASA, 57; Capstone, 9; Corbis: Bettmann, 12, 63, 65, Hulton-
Deutsch Collection, 53; Courtesy of the Naval Research Laboratory, 18;
DigitalVision, cover (moon); Getty Images Inc: MPI, 73, UIG/Sovfoto, 6; NASA,
29, 40, 43, 51, 61, 70, 75, 80, 97, 100, 105, Human Space Flight Center, 88, 93,
Kennedy Space Center Archives, 24, 76, Langley Research Center, 10, Marshall
Space Flight Center, 34, 84, 103; National Archives and Records Administration,
14, 33; Newscom: Everett Collection, 20, Itar-Tass Photos, 47; Shutterstock: Igor
Kovalchuk, cover (space background), Marcel Clemens, cover (earth)

Printed in the United States of America in Stevens Point, Wisconsin.
052014   008215R

TABLE OF CONTENTS

ABOUT YOUR ADVENTURE

YOU live in an exciting time—the space race. The Soviet Union started the race by launching the first satellite, *Sputnik*. The U.S. launched the satellite *Explorer I*, and the race was on! Who will win the race to the moon? No one knows.

In this book you'll explore how the choices people made led to a moon landing. The events you'll experience happened to real people.

Chapter One sets the scene. Then you choose which path to read. Follow the directions at the bottom of each page. The choices you make will change your outcome. After you finish one path, go back and read the others for new perspectives and more adventures.

*YOU CHOOSE the path
you take through history.*

The launch of *Sputnik* was the first leg of the space race.

Power Struggle

At the end of World War II, the United States and the Soviet Union were the strongest countries in the world. At first they were friends. But the Soviets started controlling other countries. They thought they had a right to do this.

Many of the countries didn't want to be part of the Soviet Union. So the United States tried to help them fight the Soviets. The Soviet government was furious. It threatened to attack the U.S. A war between the U.S. and the Soviet Union could destroy both countries.

7

Turn the

Neither country really wanted to start a war with guns and bombs. But each wanted to show that it was better and stronger than the other. So they fought each other indirectly. They spied on each other. They threatened to drop nuclear bombs on each other. This non-war conflict between the U.S. and the Soviet Union was called the Cold War.

The space race began in the middle of the Cold War, which was a time of mistrust and fear. The Soviet Union launched *Sputnik 1*, the world's first satellite, in 1957. The news stunned the U.S. Most Americans thought the Soviet Union was a backward country. *Sputnik* proved them wrong. It also proved that the Soviet Union had rockets that could send a nuclear bomb to the U.S.

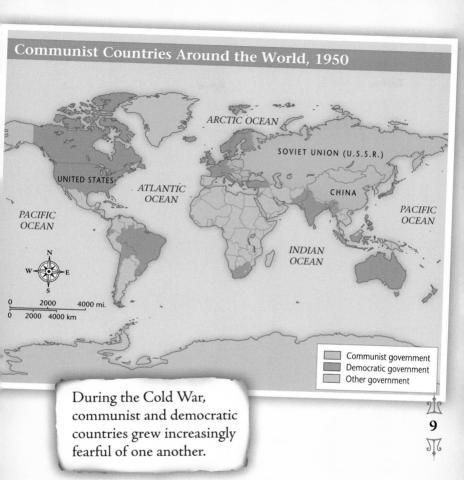

Communist Countries Around the World, 1950

ARCTIC OCEAN

SOVIET UNION (U.S.S.R.)

UNITED STATES

ATLANTIC OCEAN

CHINA

PACIFIC OCEAN

PACIFIC OCEAN

INDIAN OCEAN

N
W — E
S

0   2000   4000 mi.
0   2000 4000 km

Communist government
Democratic government
Other government

During the Cold War, communist and democratic countries grew increasingly fearful of one another.

9

Turn the p

Lunar Orbiter 1 took photos of Earth while orbiting the moon in 1966.

The space race became a symbolic contest for world power between the two countries. There were no rules in the space race. But there was a goal and there would be a winner. President John F. Kennedy set the goal—get a man on the moon by the end of 1969. The space race was on!

➤ *To be a young scientist working on early rocket technology, turn to page 13.*

➤ *To be a jet-setting reporter following the space "firsts," turn to page 41.*

➤ *To be a member of Mission Control during the 1969 moon landing, turn to page 77.*

A V-2 rocket was launched in Germany.

CHAPTER 2

Enemies Rocket to Space

The New Mexico desert stretches out in front of your small house. Before you came here from Germany, you had never seen the desert. Back then, in the early 1940s, you were a young scientist working in Peenemünde, Germany. World War II was raging. Adolf Hitler was the leader of Germany. He and his Nazi Party launched the war against many European countries. You tried not to think about the terrible things that Germany and the Nazis were doing. Instead you focused on the job in front of you: helping other German scientists build a rocket called the V-2.

13

Turn the page.

When the war ended, you expected to be arrested. To your surprise the Americans invited you to move to the United States. They wanted to build rockets, and they needed the Germans to help them. So you came to the U.S. with hundreds of other German scientists. That's how you ended up here, at the Army Ordnance Proving Ground test site, building rockets for the U.S. military.

Adolf Hitler was in power for 12 years.

When World War II ended, the Soviet Union and U.S. raced to get as much rocket technology from Germany as they could. The Americans got the V-2 rockets and a lot of scientists. The Soviets got scientists and rocket technology too. Each country is terrified that the other will get rockets into space first.

Now it's October 4, 1957, and something seems to have happened. You head to the administration building. Scientists are standing around a radio.

"What is it?" you ask. No one says anything. A strange, steady BEEP BEEP BEEP comes from the radio.

"That, gentlemen, is *Sputnik*," one scientist says. "*Sputnik* is a satellite. At this very moment, *Sputnik* is orbiting Earth. That beep is *Sputnik's* signal. The Soviets have beat us into space."

Turn the page.

Everyone knew the Soviets were close to a rocket launch. But no one realized how close. The U.S. is still months away from a similar launch. Your boss speaks up.

"The U.S. is almost ready to launch our own rocket," he says. "We've got two rocket programs. As you know, the Vanguard program has been going for a few years. Another program, the Explorer program, is about to get started. We need scientists for both programs, NOW."

➤ To volunteer for the Vanguard program, go to page 17.

➤ To volunteer for the Explorer program, turn to page 22.

Almost before you know what's happening, you're relocated to the Naval Research Laboratory in Washington, D.C. The Vanguard program was started here in 1955. Its goal is to design and build a satellite, develop a rocket to launch it, and to track the satellite once it is in orbit. Even though there have been several successful test launches, the project has had a lot of problems. Several test rockets have exploded. The hope now is that the next one, TV3, will make it to space.

The mood here is fearful, just like it was in New Mexico. If the Soviets can launch a satellite, they could attack the U.S. with nuclear missiles. The only way to fight the threat is to get an American rocket into space. Now everyone is working overtime to get Vanguard to launch.

Turn the page.

The TV3 launch is scheduled for December 6, 1957. You can stay at the lab to watch the launch. Or you can go to Cape Canaveral, Florida, to see the launch in person.

➤ To stay at the lab, go to page **19**.

➤ To go to Cape Canaveral, turn to page **31**.

Launch day is bright and clear. Television cameras are recording the event. This is a huge moment in the space race. If the TV3 is successful, the U.S. will finally have a satellite in space!

You hold your breath. The huge rocket begins to rise. But it only goes a few feet and then falls back to the ground in a huge, fiery ball of smoke and flames. The rocket is a failure. What's worse, the whole world is watching.

The country is in an uproar. President Dwight D. Eisenhower is furious. This disaster is a terrible embarrassment to the country. In a play on the word *Sputnik*, the launch is called "Flopnik" and "Oopsnik." Senator Lyndon Johnson calls it the "most humiliating failure in America's history." Now everyone wonders if the U.S. will ever launch a satellite into space.

Turn the page.

You've got a decision to make. Though you're disappointed, you can stay with the Vanguard program. But there's also the Mercury program. It's set to start in a few months. The Mercury program will choose the astronauts whom everyone hopes will someday travel in space.

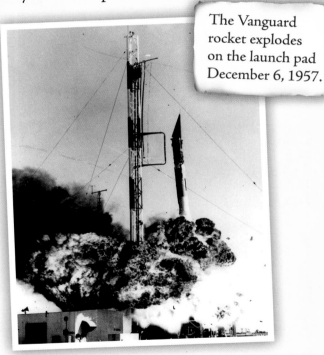

The Vanguard rocket explodes on the launch pad December 6, 1957.

➤ To stay with Vanguard, go to page **21**.

➤ To go to the Mercury program, turn to page **24**.

The TV3 disaster was bad. But now things are going well. It's March 17, 1958, and a new Vanguard is about to be launched.

Finally it's time for liftoff. The rocket carrying *Vanguard 1* sails smoothly into the air and disappears into the sky. Success! The satellite is carrying two radios and a temperature sensor. One of the radios is powered by solar energy. That is a first! The space race is neck and neck now.

You hear the government is going to start a space agency called the National Aeronautics and Space Administration. It would be great to be a part of NASA. But you miss Germany. Maybe it's time to go back.

➤ *To join the NASA Mercury program, turn to page* **24**.

➤ *To return to Germany, turn to page* **32**.

Soon you're at the Redstone Arsenal in Huntsville, Alabama. A staff member shows you around. "You'll be working with Wernher von Braun," the man says.

You know von Braun. He was head of the German rocket program at Peenemünde during World War II. After the war you both were part of the group of German scientists who came to the U.S. For a few years you both worked at White Sands, New Mexico. Von Braun and his group came to Huntsville to work on ballistic rockets in 1950.

"Were you a Nazi?" your guide asks suddenly, an unpleasant look in his eyes. It's not the first time someone's asked that question. Shaking your head you reply, "I tried to avoid the Nazis whenever possible."

Your guide shows you into von Braun's office. "My friend!" von Braun says when he sees you. "I'm so glad you are part of the team. We've already got a rocket in storage. It could have been the first rocket in space! But the government wouldn't let me use it. *Sputnik* changed everything. Now the government is going to turn us loose and let us do something!"

Von Braun says *Explorer 1* will be launched at the end of January 1958. A Jupiter-C rocket will take the satellite into orbit. The engineers also need help with *Explorer's* scientific equipment.

➤ *To work on the Jupiter-C rocket, turn to page **34**.*
➤ *To work on the scientific equipment, turn to page **36**.*

It's hard to believe that you're going to be part of history: the beginning of the U.S. space program. One of NASA's main goals is to put a person in space. That is the task of the Mercury program.

The flight director, Christopher Kraft Jr., calls the first meeting. He tells you that his boss, Chuck Mathews, has given him a simple task.

Christopher Kraft joined the National Advisory Committee for Aeronautics, the organization that preceded NASA, in 1945.

"Chris," Mathews had said, "you come up with a basic mission plan. You know, the bottom-line stuff on how we fly a man from a launch pad into space and back again. It would be good if you kept him alive."

Everyone laughs, but Kraft is serious. We have to invent everything, he says. We have to create the facility we need to do this. We have to design the networks, the tracking systems, the communications systems, the flight plans.

Suddenly you're not sure this is the job you want. It is exciting, but you've also heard about the Mercury astronaut-testing program. It might be fun to help choose the first U.S. astronauts.

➻ To join the astronaut selection team, turn to page 26.

➻ To stay in Kraft's group, turn to page 37.

The search for the first American astronauts has begun. Every candidate must be a qualified jet pilot and military test pilot, which excludes women, and have at least 1,500 hours of flying time. They have to be in excellent mental and physical shape and no older than 40. Each astronaut has to be no taller than 5 feet 11 inches. They all must have college degrees in engineering or similar fields.

Your group makes a list of 110 military men who qualify for the program. It's expected that some people will say no. Almost no one does! Finally the list is cut down to 32 men. They are asked to come in for a long list of tests.

➤ *To help with the physical tests, go to page* **27**.

➤ *To help with the stress tests, turn to page* **28**.

➤ *To help with the mental testing, turn to page* **29**.

One by one each candidate arrives for testing. They are X-rayed. Their eyes, ears, noses, and throats are checked and rechecked. The candidates go through muscle tests, water tests, and heart tests. The doctors get a complete medical history on each man, from the time he was born until today. Thirty-one candidates move on to the next series of tests.

You can help out with some of the other tests. Or you can score each candidate and bring your recommendations to the final meeting.

→ To help with the stress tests, turn to page **28**.

→ To help with the mental tests, turn to page **29**.

→ To go to the final meeting, turn to page **39**.

Flying in space puts great stress on a person's body. The tests will show whether a candidate can take it. Each man is tested on how much pressure he can stand. The men are also tested for how well they handle vibrations, loud noises, heat, and cold. Then come the endurance tests. They have to run on treadmills and be put upside down on tilt tables. Each man's feet are plunged into ice water. During one test each candidate has to blow up balloons until he is exhausted.

When the tests are over, you can help out with the other tests. Or you can finish your scores and bring your recommendations to the final meeting.

➤ *To help with the mental tests, go to page **29**.*

➤ *To go to the final meeting, turn to page **39**.*

It is vital that every astronaut be mentally ready for whatever will happen during a space flight. Each candidate spends a week with doctors and psychologists. The candidates answer question after question.

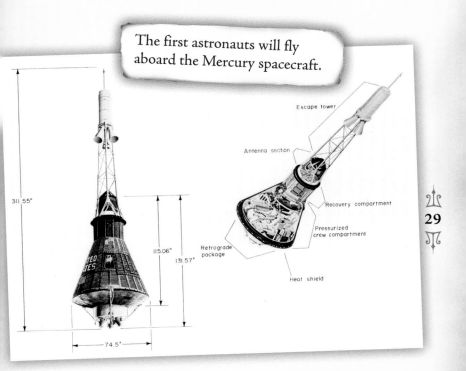

The first astronauts will fly aboard the Mercury spacecraft.

311.55"

115.06"

131.57"

74.5"

Escape tower

Antenna section

Recovery compartment

Pressurized crew compartment

Retrograde package

Heat shield

Turn the page.

Some questions seem a bit odd at first, like "who am I?" and "whom would you assign to the mission if you could not go yourself?" But the answers to the questions show what each man thinks about himself and his fellow candidates. They show whether he can be a good leader, if he can work under pressure, and if he is confident enough to face the dangers of space.

A psychologist tests the candidates on their attitudes toward fame. Everyone knows that the first American astronauts will be world famous. Their privacy will be gone. Their friends and families will have to face this fame as well. How will these men handle the pressure? You write down every answer. Soon you are ready to bring your recommendations to the final meeting.

➤ *Turn to page* **39**.

It's a cool, bright day in Florida. You, along with other scientists and engineers, are watching the launch from the viewing area, which is a safe distance from the rocket.

The engines roar to life. The rocket begins to lift off. Suddenly it pauses, then crumbles onto the pad in a big ball of fire. The U.S. will be the joke of the whole world now. You leave, convinced that the American space program is over.

THE END

To follow another path, turn to page 11.
To read the conclusion, turn to page 101.

After several weeks of difficult travel, you are finally home. It's been 13 years since the war ended, but many areas of Germany are still in shambles. The landscape is dotted with bombed-out buildings and destroyed towns. But you are happy to see that some areas have been rebuilt.

The country is divided into two parts. The German Democratic Republic (East Germany) is controlled by the Soviet Union. Thankfully, your hometown is in the Federal Republic of Germany (West Germany). It is now a free, democratic country. As you travel through the countryside, you are saddened at how much is gone. You have no idea if your parents are still alive. All your letters over the years have been returned. You are hopeful, though, that someone will know what became of your family.

THE END

To follow another path, turn to page 11.
To read the conclusion, turn to page 101.

The city of Nuremberg was heavily damaged during World War II.

The Jupiter-C rocket is a lot like the rockets you worked on in Germany during the war. Von Braun used the old V-2 designs to create the current version. Your job is to make sure the motors in it are ready to go.

One morning several men in dark suits appear in your office. "We have new evidence to suggest you were a Nazi, or you worked with Nazis, during the war," they say.

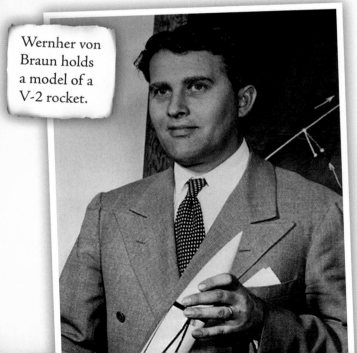

Wernher von Braun holds a model of a V-2 rocket.

You are silent. Like many other German scientists, you joined the Nazi Party to be safe. Those who didn't join could lose their jobs—or worse. There had been rumors that Jewish slave labor had built the V-2 rockets you worked on at Peenemünde. At the time you were too frightened to find out if the rumors were true. The men grill you for hours. It's no use telling them you weren't part of it. Just by being there, you were.

Finally they drop the bombshell: you are to be deported. They escort you out. It's the last time you ever see the United States.

35

THE END

To follow another path, turn to page 11.
To read the conclusion, turn to page 101.

The main mission of the satellite is to collect data from space. The *Explorer* has temperature sensors, microphones, and battery-powered transmitters. A cosmic-ray detector is designed to measure the radiation around Earth. Every day you check and recheck the instruments. After the Vanguard disaster, this launch must be perfect.

The day of the launch arrives, January 31, 1958. You hold your breath as the rocket takes off and disappears into the sky. Then something goes wrong. The tracking stations can't pick up a signal. *Explorer 1* is silent. What happened?

Everyone barely moves or speaks for eight terrible minutes. Then the word comes: they have the signal! Finally the United States has successfully entered the space race!

THE END

To follow another path, turn to page 11.
To read the conclusion, turn to page 101.

Soon the group lays out the three goals for the Mercury program: To put a manned spacecraft in orbit around Earth, to study how people can live and work in space, and to safely recover the man and the spacecraft. More than anything, you want to make the Mercury program work.

The group argues for days about how to accomplish its goals. Everyone finally decides on a few basic rules. You'll use existing technology and hardware as much as possible. Simple ideas are usually the best, so you don't want things to get too complicated. You'll develop a testing program to make sure everything works the way it's supposed to.

Turn the page.

You all also agree that the spacecraft has to have certain things, such as an easy launch escape system, some manual controls for the astronauts, rockets powerful enough to take the craft into space, and a body design that will let it land in water.

The next few months are going to be tough, but you're confident that there will be an American astronaut in space. It's a huge job for everyone, but you are ready.

THE END

To follow another path, turn to page 11.
To read the conclusion, turn to page 101.

Eighteen candidates pass all the tests. It's so tough to narrow the number of candidates that the group decides to choose seven astronauts instead of six, as originally planned.

NASA holds a press conference April 9, 1959, to introduce the Mercury Seven astronauts to the world. You stand to the side as they are called: John Glenn Jr., Scott Carpenter, Gordon Cooper Jr., Alan Shepard Jr., Gus Grissom, Walter Schirra, and Donald "Deke" Slayton. America falls in love with this handsome, confident group of men. You're proud to have helped choose them. You can't wait to see them in space. The Soviet Union doesn't have a chance now!

39

THE END

To follow another path, turn to page 11.
To read the conclusion, turn to page 101.

President John Kennedy called on the U.S. to land a man on the moon before the end of the 1960s.

CHAPTER 3

1960s: The Race Heats Up

The pressroom at the White House is crowded and hot. You are here with other journalists to report on President John Kennedy's speech today, May 25, 1961. You're a young reporter eager to land a big story.

The president is speaking before Congress. He talks about the Soviets and the head start they have in space exploration. But, he continues, "this is not merely a race. ... We go into space because whatever mankind must undertake, free men must fully share. ... First, I believe that this nation should commit itself to achieving the goal, before this decade is out, of landing a man on the moon and returning him safely to the Earth."

Turn the page.

Sending a man to the moon! If anyone can do it, it's the United States. But the Soviet Union has a big head start. On April 12, 1961, Soviet cosmonaut Yuri Gagarin orbited Earth, becoming the first person to travel in space. A few weeks later, on May 5, American astronaut Alan Shepard Jr. became the first American in space, but he didn't orbit the planet.

The next years are going to be exciting, and you want to be a part of it. You're going to write all about the space race. The first thing you want to do is to interview the only two men who have flown in space.

42

➸ *To interview Yuri Gagarin, go to page* **43**.
➸ *To meet Alan Shepard Jr., turn to page* **48**.

The Soviet Union and the U.S. fear and distrust each other. The space race has made this feeling worse. Your editor has assigned you to the Moscow office of your newspaper. After many weeks the Soviet Union finally gives permission for you to go. It won't be hard to get permission to interview Gagarin. The Soviet Union is proud of its cosmonaut.

Since Gagarin's flight in April 1961, the world has wanted to know about him. When you meet Gagarin, you're surprised how young he is. He was only 27 when he flew into space. "What was it like?" you ask.

Yuri Gagarin

Turn the page.

"It was beautiful," he says. Being weightless was strange, he adds. He played with a weightless pencil and drank water from a tube. He was only in space for 79 minutes. His capsule made just one orbit around Earth. When he came back to Earth, he landed in a farmer's field. From that moment on he was a national hero.

During the interview Gagarin mentions someone called the "chief designer." When you ask him about it, Gagarin frowns. No one is supposed to know the name of the chief designer, he tells you. He is a Soviet secret. If you could find out who the chief designer is, what a news prize that would be!

➤ To find the chief designer, go to page 45.
➤ To go back to your Moscow office, turn to page 64.

The next afternoon you find yourself in a dim office asking for permission to find the mysterious chief designer. The officer you speak to seems fearful of your questions. This designer must be very important. Maybe it wasn't a good idea to ask permission to interview him.

A few days later you are told that you cannot have permission to interview the chief designer. Now you are determined to find out more about this mysterious person. You call a few of your Soviet contacts in the government. One says he knows who the chief designer is, but he warns you against the interview. If Soviet officials find out what you are up to, you could be deported or put into prison.

➤ To interview the chief designer, turn to page **46**.

➤ To give up on finding the chief designer, turn to page **64**.

It takes some work, but you finally find the chief designer. His name is Sergei Korolev. He is happy to answer your questions.

"I have been interested in rockets since I was a young man," he says. During and after World War II, Korolev designed military rockets. Many German engineers and scientists came to the Soviet Union after the war. Korolev and his team of scientists used German technology to design and build the rocket that put *Sputnik* into space.

Right after the success of the first *Sputnik*, Korolov and his team launched *Sputnik 2* and *Sputnik 3*. *Sputnik 2* carried the first live creature into space, a dog named Laika. Then came the Luna projects. *Luna 1* was the first rocket to fly by the moon. *Luna 2* was the first spacecraft to land on the moon. *Luna 3* took the first pictures of the dark side of the moon.

"We are the best in space!" he declares. "We will win the space race and be the first to put a man on the moon!"

Korolev also tells you a secret: there are plans for another manned mission into space. "Stay in the Soviet Union for a few more weeks," he says. "You won't be disappointed."

When you leave you notice someone following you. Are you about to be arrested?

Sergei Korolev (right) with Yuri Gagarin

Turn to page **65**.

Before the interview you find out more about Alan Shepard Jr.'s historic flight. He flew 116 miles above Earth and was in the air for 15 minutes. He named the Mercury spacecraft *Freedom 7*. It flew more than 5,000 miles an hour! Shepard didn't fly as high as Gagarin, or as long, but he's still an American hero.

Shepard tells you that he was a test pilot before he was picked for the Mercury astronaut program. When you ask him what it takes to be an astronaut, he says that it takes confidence in your abilities. It's not about the fame or the glory. It's about believing that you have the talent to get the job done.

Alan Shepard in the Mercury spacecraft

There's another flight scheduled for July, Shepard tells you. Gus Grissom is going to be the second American to go into space. Shepard adds that NASA is planning a new space program, but he's not sure about the details.

↠ To report on the new space program, turn to page **50**.

↠ To watch Gus Grissom's flight, turn to page **67**.

The hotel conference room is crowded with people and reporters waiting to hear the announcement. A man stands in front of the crowd. "My name is Robert Gilruth, and I'm the head of NASA's Space Task Group," he begins. "My job is to put humans into space."

To do that, he explains, NASA must train astronauts in space. The first program, Mercury, proved that humans could survive in space. The future Apollo program will send men to the moon. But there needs to be a program in between. That program will train astronauts on how to pilot a spacecraft to the moon.

This new space program will start by putting astronauts in space for longer periods of time. It will train astronauts to dock with other space vehicles. Finally engineers and scientists will learn how to build a spacecraft that can safely travel to the moon and back.

By the next day the world knows about this new space program, called Gemini. Soon the United States will have a man, or two, in orbit! But the Soviets aren't slowing down. You've heard that the Soviets plan to shoot a female cosmonaut into space. The Soviet Union gives you permission to interview her.

Astronauts train in a Gemini simulator.

→ To meet the first woman in space, turn to page **52**.

→ To write a story about the next American in space, turn to page **56**.

Her name is Valentina Tereshkova. She's a 24-year-old factory worker. She loves to parachute out of airplanes and has made more than 100 jumps. She and three other women went through months of training. Tereshkova was chosen to be the first woman in space.

Tereshkova's spacecraft, the *Vostok 6*, launches into orbit June 16, 1963. Three days later she returns safely to Earth. Her flight makes headlines around the world.

When you meet Tereshkova, she talks about the flight and how difficult her training was. She says she felt sick during the early part of her space flight. But it was the food that made her feel ill, not the flight. She soon felt better and completed her historic trip. As you talk to her, you wonder when the United States will have a female astronaut.

Valentina Tereshkova was chosen from more than 400 applicants for her mission in space.

→To stay and report on the Soviet space program, turn to page **54**.

→To go back to the United States, turn to page **59**.

The next big challenge for the Soviet space program is a space walk. No one has ever left a craft while it's in space. For the next two years the Soviets work and train so they can be the first to complete a space walk.

It's now March 18, 1965. Cosmonauts Alexei Leonov and Pavel Belyayev blast into orbit aboard the *Voskhod 2*. When they are in space, Leonov puts on his suit and slowly opens the hatch. He is floating in space! Leonov floats in space for about 10 minutes before slowly returning to the ship.

When the cosmonauts get back to Earth, you are given permission to interview Leonov.

"How did it feel to walk in space?" you ask.

"Like a seagull with its wings outstretched, soaring high above the Earth," he says. But there were problems too. He almost didn't get back inside the spacecraft! His suit was so stiff that he couldn't move his arms or legs. He had to release some of the oxygen in his suit so he could move. It became a race to get back inside the ship before his oxygen ran out.

It's great that you got to interview Leonov. But you're starting to get homesick. You haven't seen the United States in two years. It's time to go home and report on the U.S. space program.

Turn to page 59.

Your story appears on the front page of the newspaper.

FIRST U.S. ASTRONAUT ORBITS EARTH

Cape Canaveral, Florida, Feb. 20, 1962—U.S. astronaut John Glenn became the first American to orbit Earth today. During his nearly five-hour trip he traveled about 81,000 miles. His capsule, *Friendship* 7, traveled at about 17,530 miles an hour. Glenn made three trips around Earth before splashing down. His historic journey was watched on television by the entire country. Much of the rest of the world tuned in for the radio broadcast of his flight.

Glenn had contact with the
ground crew through the trip. One
of the first things he said was
"Oh, that view is tremendous." As
he flew over the Canary Islands,
Glenn described the horizon as "a
brilliant blue."

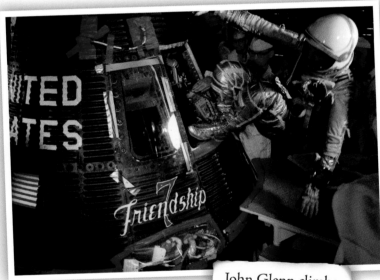

John Glenn climbs
into *Friendship 7*.

Turn the page.

The Project Mercury team was worried that *Friendship* 7 might break apart when it fell to Earth. Everyone was relieved when it held up magnificently.

Today is being called one of the greatest days in space for the United States. Glenn's space flight wasn't as long as Soviet cosmonaut Gherman Titov's flight that began on August 6, 1961. But to the world, this trip has helped the United States gain ground in the space race.

Your editor loves the story and keeps you on the space beat. You spend your time learning all you can about the space program.

To cover the Gemini missions, go to page **59**.

To interview astronaut Gordon Cooper, turn to page **69**.

The space race is moving so fast it's hard to believe how far the U.S. has come since President Kennedy made his challenge to reach the moon. You can hardly believe the interesting stories you are covering. American astronauts Gus Grissom and John Young flew in the first two-man Gemini mission. The U.S. finally got its own spacewalker on June 3, 1965, when Ed White made his historic walk. In December two American astronauts, Frank Borman and James Lovell, stayed in orbit for two weeks aboard *Gemini 7*.

Turn the page.

The space race sped up even more in 1966. In February the Soviet craft *Luna 9* was the first spacecraft to land on the moon. Two months later *Luna 10* was the first satellite to orbit the moon. The U.S. wasn't far behind. In June *Surveyor 1* landed on the moon. A few weeks later, *Lunar Orbiter 1* orbited the moon and took the first pictures of Earth from the moon.

American scientists and astronauts are even more determined to get to the moon since President Kennedy's assassination three years ago. They want to honor the president who had the vision to challenge the United States to go there.

Now it's the end of 1966. The Gemini program is winding down, and the Apollo program is getting started. You can go to the *Apollo 1* training center and interview the astronauts who will go to the moon. Or you can write about the last Gemini flight.

The *Luna 9* was the first spacecraft to send photos to Earth of the lunar surface.

❧ To go to the training center, turn to page **62**.

❧ To report on the last Gemini flight, turn to page **70**.

It's January 27, 1967. The Apollo training center is buzzing with activity. Today will be a simulation. The three astronauts doing the practice flight are Gus Grissom, Ed White, and Roger Chaffee. They're aboard *Apollo 1*. You're hoping to interview them later.

The three astronauts climb into the craft and strap in. Some problems delay the start of the simulation. You're taking notes when suddenly one of the astronaut's voices shouts over the radio: "I've got a fire in the cockpit!"

Everyone freezes, horrified, watching a video monitor. A bright light bursts inside the module. A few seconds later, you hear a loud explosion. Someone yells, "Get them out of there!" Several men rush to help the astronauts. But the heat and smoke drive them away. When they finally get the capsule open, it's clear that none of the astronauts survived.

No one knows what happened. You want to investigate the accident. Your editor says no. He wants you to write about other missions.

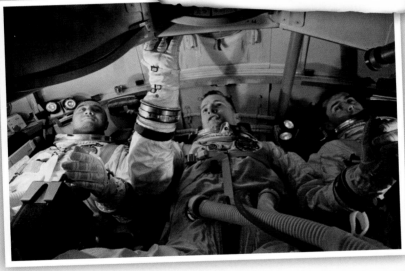

Roger Chaffee (from left), Ed White, and Gus Grissom died almost instantly when their craft caught fire.

➤ To find out what happened on Apollo 1, turn to page 72.

➤ To follow other missions, turn to page 74.

It's too risky to defy the Soviet government, no matter how much you want to find the chief designer. While you are on the street, several Soviet officers surround you. No one will tell you what you've done, but you are sure it has to do with asking permission to interview the chief designer.

You're taken to a police station. Then you're put into a cell. After several hours of questions you are finally released. That was a close call. Some people who end up in Soviet prisons are never seen again.

THE END

To follow another path, turn to page 11.
To read the conclusion, turn to page 101.

Days pass, and no one comes for you. Your editor agrees to let you cover the next Soviet manned space flight. Finally in August 1961, you hear that Gagarin's friend and fellow cosmonaut Gherman Titov is about to go into orbit.

Titov is shot into space on August 6. You and the rest of the Soviet Union see him on Soviet TV smiling inside his capsule. After one day and 17 orbits around Earth, Titov lands safely—the second man in space! The Soviet people are wild with joy.

Gherman Titov was the second cosmonaut to orbit Earth.

Turn the page.

At the press conference a few days later, you question Titov. He tells you he was the first person ever to sleep in space. At first he had trouble because his arms would rise up into the air and wake him up. So he slid his hands under the belt of his chair to hold them down. Then he could sleep. But when he woke up, his hands were in the air again.

When you get back to your desk, the boss has some bad news. The Soviets found out about your interview with Korolev. You are being deported! Sadly you pack your things and head for the airport. Your adventure in the Soviet Union is over.

THE END

To follow another path, turn to page 11.
To read the conclusion, turn to page 101.

The mood at Cape Canaveral is tense. Bad weather delayed the launch twice. Finally on July 21, everything looks good. "Three, two, one, liftoff!" Gus Grissom's rocket sails into the sky.

Grissom is in space for only 15 minutes. You watch the TV monitors as his capsule drops into the ocean about 300 miles off the Florida coast. Then the capsule disappears beneath the waves.

"The capsule has sunk!" someone cries. "It looks like the hatch opened too soon."

Soon word comes: Grissom got out of the capsule before it sank. The astronaut is safe! Everyone cheers with relief.

Turn the page.

Later you write a story about the launch. Your editor loves it. But he has some bad news. "I'm taking you off the space beat," he says. "You can still write about the space program, but you'll be doing other stories too."

This is disappointing news. The space race is exciting, and you like being a part of it. But there are other news stories to cover, and you look forward to writing about the wall that is going up in Berlin, Germany, and the growing tensions between the U.S. and Cuba.

THE END

To follow another path, turn to page 11.
To read the conclusion, turn to page 101.

It's May 1963 and the space race has blasted full speed ahead since John Glenn made his historic orbit. Now you're about to meet Gordon Cooper, the American astronaut who completed a 34-hour space flight—and the last solo flight any American astronaut would make.

Cooper grins and shakes your hand. "Call me Gordo," he says. Soon he's telling you all about his flight. One of his favorite things was the view of Earth. There's nothing like being an astronaut, he says.

Later as you're driving home, you think about the interview. It's dark, and the moon is bright. You wonder what it would be like for a person to see Earth from the moon. Someday, maybe, that will happen.

THE END

To follow another path, turn to page 11.
To read the conclusion, turn to page 101.

The world is so excited about the upcoming Apollo missions that the last Gemini mission, *Gemini 12*, seems like an afterthought. It launches and returns safely, but everyone is focused on the moon. The Gemini launch pad equipment is already being torn down to get ready for Apollo. You're the only reporter in the room when astronauts Jim Lovell and Edwin "Buzz" Aldrin Jr. sit down.

The *Gemini 7* and *Gemini 6* were the first to rendezvous in space.

"It was the last Gemini, and we got it all right," Lovell says. Aldrin nods. He tells you that his spacewalk lasted more than two hours and went perfectly. Now the two astronauts are looking forward to going to the moon.

As the two men leave, you remember something that President Lyndon Johnson said. "Early in 1962, John Glenn made his historic orbital flight and America was in space. Now, nearly five years later, we have completed Gemini, and we know that America is in space to stay."

71

THE END

To follow another path, turn to page 11.
To read the conclusion, turn to page 101.

During the investigation NASA officials discover that several things went wrong. The cockpit was filled with pure oxygen, which can catch fire easily. A wire under Gus Grissom's seat was not covered correctly. When he moved in his seat, the wire likely sparked. That started the fire. The astronauts couldn't get the hatch open fast enough to save themselves.

The horrible accident forces NASA to make changes to the space program. They make sure most of the items in space are not flammable. They no longer put pure oxygen into the cockpit. The wiring systems are redesigned so they won't cause sparks. All the changes put the whole space program on hold.

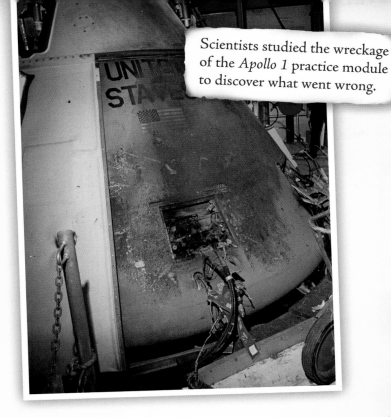

Scientists studied the wreckage of the *Apollo 1* practice module to discover what went wrong.

Some people think the accident will stop the space program from getting to the moon. You don't think so. There will be an American on the moon before the decade is out, just like President Kennedy promised.

THE END

To follow another path, turn to page 11.
To read the conclusion, turn to page 101.

It's been almost two years since the horrible *Apollo 1* accident. The Apollo program recovered and sent several unmanned missions into space. *Apollo 8* is the big one. Three astronauts will be orbiting the moon! *Apollo 8* launches on December 21, 1968. It's a practice run for landing a man on the moon.

Everything goes perfectly. It takes *Apollo 8* three days to get to the moon. For 20 hours the astronauts orbit the moon 10 times, taking photos and doing experiments. You're listening to their broadcast on Christmas Eve, just like the rest of the world. After reading from the Bible, the crew says, "Good night, good luck, a Merry Christmas, and God bless all of you—all of you on the good Earth."

It's the beginning of a new age of human space exploration. You feel lucky that you're alive to witness it.

Images of the moon's surface were taken during the *Apollo 8* mission.

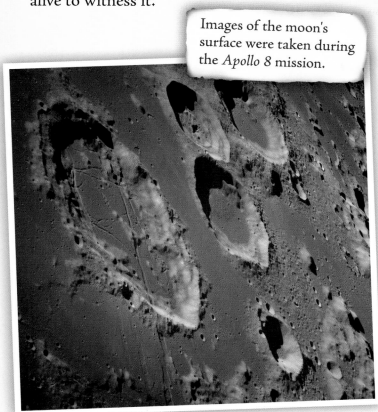

THE END

To follow another path, turn to page 11.
To read the conclusion, turn to page 101.

Apollo 11 heads for space.

CHAPTER 4

Finish Line: The Moon!

It's July 16, 1969. After years of work, tests, terrible failures, and wild successes, *Apollo 11* is about to begin its journey to the moon. You're part of the Mission Control team that will work to get astronauts Neil Armstrong, Edwin "Buzz" Aldrin Jr., and Michael Collins there.

The Mission Control parking lot is full, even this early in the morning. Everyone is here for the launch. Later some people will go home while others stay. The whole moon trip will take about eight days, so everyone works in shifts.

77

Turn the page.

The rocket's engines roar to life at 9:32 a.m. Enormous bursts of flame spread across the launch pad. "Five, four, three, two, one, we have liftoff!" The giant rocket lifts into the sky. Soon the astronauts are barreling toward the moon at more than 24,000 miles per hour.

Everyone in Mission Control has a job to do. You can help the team that will land the astronauts on the moon. Or you can work with the team that will launch the lunar module from the moon for the first phase of the return trip home.

➤ *To work with the landing team, go to page* **79**.
➤ *To work with the return trip team, turn to page* **88**.

In three days the astronauts will reach the moon. Until then the landing team goes over every detail again and again. No one wants to miss something when it's time to land on the moon.

Landing day is July 20. Neil Armstrong and Buzz Aldrin are in the lunar module, which is headed for the surface. Michael Collins is in the larger command module that will orbit the moon.

The flight director, Gene Kranz, greets everyone on the team. Later he calls everyone on the private communication channel.

"Listen up," he says. "Today is our day, and the hopes and the dreams of the entire world are with us. … In the next hour we will do something that has never been done before. We will land an American on the moon. … Good luck and God bless us today!"

Turn the page.

As soon as Kranz is finished speaking, communication with the lunar module goes out!

Buzz Aldrin adjusts his headset as he works inside the lunar module.

➤ To try to get communication back, go to page **81**.

➤ To wait and hope communication resumes on its own, turn to page **96**.

"Problem with communication," you report immediately. "We can talk to the astronauts, but we don't have systems communication."

"We need data from the lunar module for landing," a crisp voice replies. Communication comes back long enough to get some data from Neil Armstrong. They're on track for landing. Then the system goes dead again.

You have an idea. "If the antennae on the lunar module is adjusted, we'll get the signal back," you say.

The message is relayed to the astronauts. Armstrong moves the module in space slightly, and the signal comes back. It's still full of static, but it's clear enough to get the information you need for landing.

"Is everything 'go' for landing?" Kranz asks.

Turn the page.

"Go," you say, relieved.

There is no time to relax. The lunar module is only a few thousand feet from the moon's surface. Suddenly two more problems appear on the consoles. Astronaut Buzz Aldrin's voice says, "We have an alarm up here."

A voice comes over the console as well: "Radar control says the lunar module is not where it's supposed to be. It's going to land in the wrong place."

➥ *To work on the alarm, go to page* **83**.

➥ *To find out what's happened with the navigation, turn to page* **85**.

"It's a 1202 alarm," someone says. That means the lunar module's computer is overloaded with information. If it gets too overloaded, it will shut down. If the computer shuts down, all the systems on the lunar module will go down too. The module would basically turn off, and the astronauts would crash to the moon's surface.

But there's a chance that the computer won't overload enough to shut down. You only have a few seconds to recommend an "Abort" or a "Go."

➤ *To continue with the mission, turn to page* **84**.

➤ *To recommend aborting the mission, turn to page* **97**.

Even though the computer's alarm is going off, everything seems to be working fine. You're getting data. The navigation and guidance systems are good. The engines are on line. When you tell Kranz about the problem, you suggest feeding some of the lunar module's workload to Mission Control's computer systems. As soon as that's done, the alarm stops. A few more alarms go off, but you're confident that everything is a go.

Engineers monitored a mission at the Kennedy Space Flight Center control room.

➤ *Turn to page 87.*

One look at the radar data, and it's clear. The lunar module has overshot its planned landing site. This is serious. The moon's surface is covered with craters, mounds, rocks, and boulders. The landing site was specifically chosen because it is smooth and flat. If the astronauts miss it, there may not be another place to land safely.

Neil Armstrong is flying the lunar module manually. The astronauts are looking for a place to land. Everyone in Mission Control goes eerily quiet.

Five hundred feet from the surface. Two hundred fifty feet from the surface. You watch the monitors and grip the edge of your seat.

Turn the page.

The lunar module is flying over a boulder field. There's nowhere it can land! The radar crew doesn't have any idea where the lunar module is, so they can't help. It's all up to Armstrong.

Then it dawns on you that they're burning extra fuel. If they run out of fuel before they find a landing spot, they'll crash. "Fuel at low level," comes a voice over the console.

The module is flying over the moon's surface, as the astronauts look for a landing spot. "They've probably got just 30 seconds of fuel," someone says.

A voice comes from the lunar module. "Forty feet, picking up some dust. Thirty feet, we're seeing a shadow." Then the words everyone has been waiting to hear crackle over the system. "Houston, Tranquility Base here. The Eagle has landed."

You didn't realize you had been holding your breath. "Roger you, Tranquility," a voice replies. "We copy you on the ground. You've got a bunch of guys about to turn blue. We're breathing again. Thanks a lot."

Your work isn't done yet. You have to recheck all the systems again, making sure everything is working properly. You go through your checklist. Everything looks great. "We're a go," you say, along with the rest of the team. Your countrymen are on the moon.

87

THE END

To follow another path, turn to page 11.
To read the conclusion, turn to page 101.

You stick around and watch the moon landing a few days later. Hundreds of millions of people watch their TVs as Neil Armstrong climbs down the lunar module ladder and steps onto the moon's surface. "That's one small step for a man, one giant leap for mankind," he says.

Over the next hours, the astronauts conduct experiments, collect moon rocks and moon dust, and plant an American flag on the moon's surface.

Neil Armstrong worked at the modular equipment storage area of the lunar module.

Armstrong and Aldrin leave a few things on the moon's surface. One is a patch from the tragic *Apollo 1* mission that never got to the moon. Another is a medal honoring Yuri Gagarin, the Russian cosmonaut and first man in space. They also leave a small gold pin shaped like an olive branch, to represent peace.

After 22 hours on the moon, it's time to come home. The lunar module will blast off from the moon. Then it will dock with the command module, which has been orbiting the moon.

You know that the lunar module didn't land where it was supposed to. In fact, no one is sure where it is! But before the lunar module can go anywhere, the astronauts have to go through their prelaunch checklist.

➤*To go through the final checklist for liftoff, turn to page* **90**.

➤*To help the team find the lunar module, turn to page* **91**.

You go through the launch checklist with Aldrin. He tells you that a switch is broken. It's the switch that will turn on the engines. No one is sure how that happened. Maybe Aldrin hit it with his backpack while he was moving around in the module. It's a good thing there's a backup system in place. But the backup system has to be turned on manually. If you use the backup system, liftoff will be delayed.

➵ *To tell Aldrin to use the backup system, turn to page **93**.*

➵ *To tell Aldrin to try the switch, turn to page **94**.*

You must find out where the lunar module is, so it can lift off at the right time to dock with the command module. Everyone has a different answer. The data from the lunar module doesn't match the data from the radar team. The backup guidance system's data doesn't match either one of them. You're not sure how to solve this problem. But you have to solve it, fast. So you decide to ask the astronauts for help.

→ *To ask Buzz Aldrin for help, turn to page* **92**.

→ *To ask Michael Collins for help, turn to page* **95**.

Maybe Aldrin can use his radar to track the command module as it flies overhead. If you can get its location and flight path, you can match it with data from the lunar module. Then it will be simple to figure out where the lunar module is.

It works! You discover that the lunar module is about four miles from where it was supposed to have landed. When you relay the information to Kranz, he's pleased. It's a go for lifting off the moon.

➤ *Turn to page* **98**.

No one agrees with your idea to use the backup system. Even Aldrin thinks he can use a pen to flip the switch. You don't want to take that chance, so you argue. If the switch doesn't work, the whole liftoff could be aborted. The thought makes you sick to your stomach. All you can do is hope everyone else is right.

An astronaut's view of the moon through the lunar module window.

→ Turn to page 98.

Aldrin thinks he can press the switch with a pen. It doesn't sound too safe, but you're going to trust Aldrin. He's the one in the module, after all.

There's only one chance to do this right. If the lunar module doesn't lift off at exactly the right time, the astronauts could float away in space. This risk is so real that the president has even prepared a speech just in case. Not many people know that. You hope no one has to find out.

➤ *Turn to page* **98**.

Michael Collins is orbiting the moon. You tell him to use a telescope to look for the lunar module on the moon's surface. He spends hours trying to find the module. He can't find it. Finally he has to focus on his own jobs.

You've failed. You know someone else on the team will find the exact location of the lunar module. Leaving the astronauts stranded on the moon is not an option. But there's no more for you to do now.

95

THE END

To follow another path, turn to page 11.
To read the conclusion, turn to page 101.

You're not worried. Communication usually comes back in a few seconds. But all you hear is static. Sometimes it stops long enough to get data, and then communication is lost again.

Eventually someone figures out that it could be the antennae on the lunar module. You listen in as Neil Armstrong adjusts the lunar module in space. Suddenly communication is back!

You're happy, but your boss is not. You didn't act quickly enough to solve the problem. Every job is critical, and one mess-up could be fatal. You will be extra careful for the rest of the day.

THE END

To follow another path, turn to page 11.
To read the conclusion, turn to page 101.

Kranz looks sternly at you when you recommend aborting the mission.

"Are all the systems working?" he asks. "Is the guidance and navigation on track? Are the module engines still running? Are we still getting data?"

You nod.

"If all the mission critical jobs are working, then we do not abort," he says. "You are relieved of your duties."

The lunar module was jammed with displays and controls.

THE END

To follow another path, turn to page 11.
To read the conclusion, turn to page 101.

Before they leave the moon forever, Armstrong describes what the surface looks like. "We're in a smooth crater field with circular craters. … The ground is very fine sand or silt. … In the ground are rocks of all shapes and sizes. … We're in a boulder field, the boulders are up to two feet with some larger than that."

"Tranquility, Houston, Roger. Very fine description."

Finally everything is ready.

"Tranquility Base, this is Houston."

"Roger, go ahead," Aldrin's voice crackles over the speakers.

"You're cleared for takeoff."

Aldrin replies, "Roger. Understand. We're number one on the runway!"

You chuckle at the joke. Aldrin uses a pen to push the switch, and it works. The engine roars to life. The module bursts away from the landing gear and quickly flies upward. Then you hear an astronaut's voice.

"The Eagle has wings."

Some time later they dock safely with the command module. It will take about three days for the return trip. When the astronauts get back, there will be parades and celebrations. You and the rest of Mission Control will be hailed as heroes. For now, though, you're just proud of the job you've done. The astronauts are safe and on their way home. The space race is over, and the U.S. has won.

THE END

To follow another path, turn to page 11.
To read the conclusion, turn to page 101.

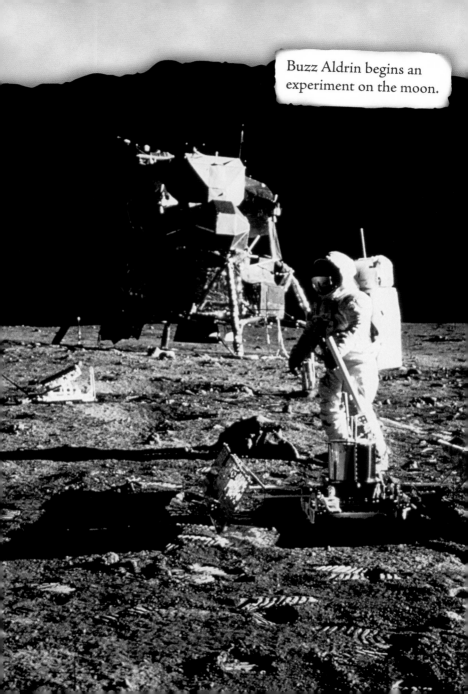

Buzz Aldrin begins an experiment on the moon.

To the Moon and Beyond

The space race only lasted 12 years. The year 1957 marked the start, when *Sputnik 1*'s "BEEP BEEP" was heard on radios around the world. The U. S. won the space race in 1969 when Neil Armstrong stepped on the moon. For most of the race, the Soviet Union was ahead. Why didn't the Soviets beat the U.S. to the moon?

The biggest reason is that chief designer Sergei Korolev died in 1966. Many people think that if Korolev had lived, the Soviets would have beaten the U.S. to the moon. After Korolev's death, the Soviet program fell apart. The government wasn't willing to pay for the space program. The rocket that was to take a cosmonaut to the moon failed several tests.

But no one in the United States knew any of this at the time. The Soviet Union kept its space program a secret from the world. The Soviets only told the world about their successes. American scientists thought the Soviets were moving forward just as fast as they were to get a man on the moon. By the time Armstrong set foot on the moon's surface, it was clear that the U.S. was far ahead.

Many of the first American astronauts continued to fly in space after *Apollo 11*. John Glenn, one of the original Mercury Seven, returned to space in 1998 and added another first to his list—as the world's oldest astronaut!

Valentina Tereshkova, the world's first woman in space, became a Soviet hero and continues to support the Soviet space program. Yuri Gagarin was killed in a plane crash in 1968. German scientist Wernher von Braun continued to work for the space program and even appeared in space films for Walt Disney. He died in 1977.

Wernher von Braun

By the 1970s the U.S. had made several more successful moon trips. The Soviet program recovered and focused on building space stations. The Soviets put the first, *Salyut 1*, into space in 1971. The U.S. sent the Skylab space station into orbit in 1973.

By the 1980s the Cold War was all but over. The Soviet Union collapsed in 1989. The countries once controlled by the Soviet Union were free. The U.S. and Russia were friendly once again. In the 1980s the International Space Station and the space shuttle programs were successful. Today the U.S. space program focuses on long-distance exploration, including sending unmanned craft to Mars.

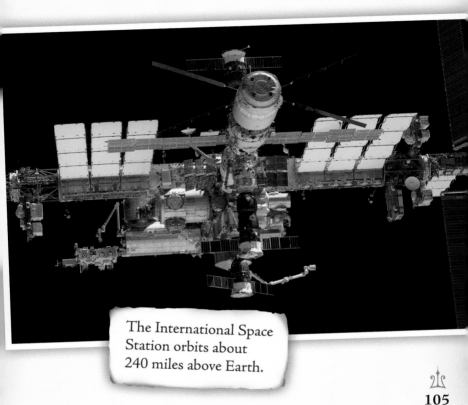

The International Space Station orbits about 240 miles above Earth.

Countries such as China, Japan, and India are sending their first satellites and crafts into space. For them the space race is just beginning.

Timeline

October 4, 1957—The Soviet Union launches *Sputnik 1,* beginning the space race.

November 3, 1957—*Sputnik 2* carries a dog named Laika into space.

December 6, 1957—The American Vanguard TV3 crashes on liftoff.

January 31, 1958—The first American satellite, *Explorer 1,* is launched.

July 29, 1958—The National Aeronautics and Space Administration (NASA) is created.

April 9, 1959—The American Mercury Seven astronauts are introduced to the world.

April 12, 1961—Soviet cosmonaut Yuri Gagarin is the first human in space.

May 5, 1961—Alan Shepard Jr. is the first American in space.

February 20, 1962—American John Glenn orbits Earth three times.

June 16, 1963—Soviet Valentina Tereshkova is the first woman in space.

March 18, 1965—Alexei Leonov of the Soviet Union performs the first spacewalk.

March 23, 1965—Gus Grissom and John Young are launched with the first manned Gemini spacecraft.

June 3, 1965—Ed White is the first American to perform a spacewalk.

February 3, 1966—*Luna 9* is the first spacecraft to soft land on the moon.

June 2, 1966—The U.S.'s *Surveyor 1* soft lands on the moon.

January 27, 1967—Gus Grissom, Ed White, and Roger Chaffee die during an *Apollo 1* test.

December 21, 1968—Frank Borman, James Lovell, and William Anders begin the first manned mission to the moon.

July 20, 1969—Neil Armstrong and Buzz Aldrin are the first people to walk on the moon.

Other Paths to Explore

In this book you've seen how the events surrounding the space race look different from several points of view.

Perspectives on history are as varied as the people who lived it. You can explore other paths on your own to learn more about what happened. Seeing history from many points of view is an important part of understanding it. Here are ideas for other points of view to explore:

+ Why was the race to space between the United States and the Soviet Union considered part of the Cold War? What is the difference between a cold war and one fought with weapons? (Common Core: Key Ideas and Details)

+ If you took the path of the reporter who interviewed the chief designer of the Soviet Union's space program, what were the possible outcomes? Why do you think you would get warned against it, and what would go into your decision to persevere? (Common Core: Craft and Structure)

+ Most of the Soviet space program, including failures, was kept secret from the public. In the U.S. the space program was widely followed by the public. Even failures such as rocket crashes were in the news. What were the advantages of keeping space disasters secret? Why would it be a good idea to make everything, even failures, known to the rest of the world? (Common Core: Integration of Knowledge and Ideas)

READ MORE

Benoit, Peter. *The Space Race.* New York: Children's Press, 2012.

Dell, Pamela. *Man on the Moon: How a Photograph Made Anything Seem Possible.* Mankato, Minn.: Compass Point Books, 2011.

Ottaviani, Jim. *T-Minus: The Race to the Moon.* New York: Aladdin, 2009.

INTERNET SITES

109

Use FactHound to find Internet sites related to this book. All of the sites on FactHound have been researched by our staff.

Here's all you do:
Visit *www.facthound.com*
Type in this code: 9781476541853

GLOSSARY

launch (LAWNCH)—to send a rocket or spacecraft into space

mission (MISH-uhn)—a planned job or task

Nazi (NOT-see)—a member of the National Socialist German Workers' Party led by Adolf Hitler that controlled Germany before and during World War II (1939–1945)

orbit (OR-bit)—the path an object follows as it goes around the sun or a planet

radiation (ray-dee-AY-shuhn)—tiny particles sent out from radioactive material

satellite (SAT-uh-lite)—an object that moves around a planet or other cosmic body

soft land (SAWFT LAND)—to land slowly without a jarring impact

transmitter (transs-MIT-uhr)—a device that converts sound waves to electrical impulses

BIBLIOGRAPHY

Brzezinski, Matthew. *Red Moon Rising: Sputnik and the Hidden Rivalries That Ignited the Space Age.* New York: Times Books, 2007.

Burgess, Colin, and Rex Hall. *The First Soviet Cosmonaut Team: Their Lives, Legacy, and Historical Impact.* Chichester, U.K.: Praxis Pub., 2009.

Chaikin, Andrew. *Mission Control, This Is Apollo: The Story of the First Voyages to the Moon.* New York: Viking, 2009.

Collins, Martin, ed. *After Sputnik: 50 Years of the Space Age.* New York: Smithsonian Books/Collins, 2007.

French, Francis, and Colin Burgess. *In the Shadow of the Moon: A Challenging Journey to Tranquility 1965–1969.* Lincoln: University of Nebraska Press, 2007.

Heppenheimer, T.A. *Countdown: A History of Space Flight.* New York: John Wiley and Sons, 1997.

Kraft, Christopher C. *Flight: My Life in Mission Control.* New York: Dutton, 2001.

Kranz, Gene. *Failure is Not an Option: Mission Control from Mercury to Apollo 13 and Beyond.* New York: Simon and Schuster, 2000.

INDEX